To Ellen

Praying you discover
God's plan,
Diane Hannay

WHAT IS GOD'S PLAN FOR ME?

A GOSPEL CONVERSATION FOR YOUNG CHILDREN

WRITTEN BY
DIANE HANNAY, M.ED.

ILLUSTRATED BY
SCARLET VANDENBOS

What is God's Plan for Me? a gospel conversation for young children

Publisher's Cataloging-in-Publication Data
Names: Hannay, Diane, author. | Vanderbos, Scarlet, illustrator.
Title: What is God's Plan for Me? A Gospel Conversation for Young Children Diane Hannay, M.Ed.; Scarlet Vanderbos.
Description: Redmond, OR: Diane Hannay, 2020.
Identifiers:
LCCN: 2020917077
ISBN: 978-1-7354791-2-5 (Hardcover)
978-1-7354791-1-8 (Paperback)
978-1-7354791-0-1 (E-Book)
Subjects: LCSH Bible stories, English. | Christian life--Juvenile literature.
BISAC JUVENILE NONFICTION / Religious / Christian / General | JUVENILE NONFICTION Religious / Christian / Devotional & Prayer
Classification: LCC BS551.2 .H345 2020 | DDC 220.9/505--dc23

For my children, Abigail and Luke, and my future grandchildren. I also dedicate this book to my nieces and nephews and their children; the students I have taught at Helderberg Christian School in New York and Central Christian School in Oregon; and the children I have and will encounter in church and in life. I pray this book will help you know the great love Jesus has for you!

Psalm 78:4, "We will not hide them from their children; we will tell the next generation the praiseworthy deeds of the LORD, his power, and the wonders he has done."

- Diane

For my sons, Rowan and Vincent, who have taught me more about God than they will ever know.

- Scarlet

TO THE ADULT...

WHAT IS GOD'S PLAN FOR ME?

was written out of a sincere love for all the children I have encountered in my life. Like you, I have a deep love for the hearts of children. As an educator and mom, it is my hope that every child I have taught, loved, and prayed for would come to understand the biblical gospel message. The gospel is not really a plan; it's a person. It's a living, vibrant relationship with the person of Jesus Christ! The only way to salvation is through faith in Him alone. The message of the whole Bible is Jesus.

SPIRITUAL GUIDE

In the back of this book is a guide to assist adults with engaging children in further spiritual conversations and understanding. Because the message of the gospel can include unfamiliar words for children to process, definitions of challenging spiritual vocabulary are provided. Two suggested prayers and a reference guide of Bible verses that support each page in *What is God's Plan for Me?* are included as additional tools.

EDUCATIONAL GUIDE

Many beautiful illustrations throughout *What is God's Plan for Me?* are based on special Central Oregon geography, flora, and fauna. As you read the book, see if you can identify the Three Sisters Mountains, Deschutes River, Smith Rock State Park, a Western Juniper tree and others. Look for the educational guide in the back of this book to assist in educational connections. Children are encouraged to search and find each unique creation of God.

SEARCH AND FIND PETS

There are two special pets illustrated throughout *What is God's Plan for Me?* Pinky and Buckshot are intentionally added in honor of the Hannay family pets. These pets hold a special place in the hearts of the author's family, as they enjoyed many adventures together. The pets moved into eight different homes over the span of sixteen years, including a dramatic move from upstate New York to Oregon. The pets' presence and maturity (take note they start as a kitten and puppy and mature to full grown animals) in the story is a significant reminder God can provide comfort through His creation as children grapple with the beauty and mystery of the gospel message throughout their lives. Search and find the pets on most of the story pages.

I hope you enjoy each personal touch shared throughout
What is God's Plan for Me?

God is the Heavenly Father and the Creator of all things.
He created everything around you like the trees, the mountains,
and even the amazing butterfly. God created the whole world.

Animals are an important part of God's creation. Can you find
the kitty, named Pinky, and the puppy, named Buckshot, on this
page? Do you have any pets? What are their names? God
gave us animals to enjoy.

God's most wonderful creation, however, is you! You are special
and unique, made in His image. Only people are made in God's
image. He made you to love and care like Him. He sent His Son,
Jesus, to show you the way.

GOD HAS A PLAN FOR YOU! This book tells that story. Follow Pinky and Buckshot through the pages as they help you answer the question, *"What is God's Plan for Me?"*

What do you see on this page? This yellow castle reminds us of the beautiful place called heaven. Heaven is real. It is a perfect place with streets of gold, gates of pearls, and lots of happiness. There will be no tears, no sickness, no pain, no death, no shame, no fear, and no darkness in heaven!

Heaven is God's home. GOD HAS A PLAN FOR YOU! He loves you and wants you to live in heaven forever with Him someday. He is even creating a special place there just for you. Heaven will be filled with peace, love, and joy. It will be more wonderful than we can imagine! Can you describe a place that you have been that was beautiful?

Place your hand on the big, dirty, broken heart. Do you think this heart was made to be dirty and torn up? No, it changed! We know this because of the Bible. God gave us His written words in the Bible. The Bible is completely true. We can trust it. The wonderful thing about the Bible is everyone can read it and know God's plan.

The Bible explains God created everyone and everything perfect in the beginning. There was no guilt, shame, or fear until the first people chose to disobey God. This is called sin. Sin is anything we do that disobeys God. When the first people sinned, they were sent away from God. Sin changed everything on Earth.

After the first people sinned, everyone was born with sin in our lives. Sin separates us from God. Sin hurts God and hurts us. It does not honor God. That is why this heart is dirty and sad. The Bible says there is NO sin in heaven. Can you think of an example of sin?

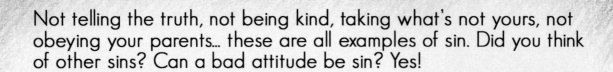

Not telling the truth, not being kind, taking what's not yours, not obeying your parents... these are all examples of sin. Did you think of other sins? Can a bad attitude be sin? Yes!

Sin creates a problem in our story. God wants us to be with Him in the beautiful place called heaven. But all people do wrong things sometimes - even you and me. Though we do good things too, like loving others and being kind, we all still sin. Can you think of a time you have done something God calls sin?

How can kids and grown-ups get to heaven if heaven doesn't allow sin? No matter how good we try to act, we cannot be good enough to get into heaven. Our sin is the problem that separates us from God.

But don't be afraid. GOD HAS A PLAN FOR YOU! He made a way to remove sin's shame. When we want to know how to live now and how to get to heaven someday, the Bible tells us. God's words give us hope.

God sent His Son, Jesus, to earth to save us from our sin. The Christmas story tells how Jesus was born and why He came to earth. Do you remember that story and can you share something you remember about it? Christmas is a wonderful time of year.

Jesus was once your age. He knows what it is like to be you - growing up with family, friends, and feelings. But He was also different than you. As God's Son, Jesus did many wonderful miracles when He was an adult. He showed people He loved them, and He told them about God His Father. No other person ever lived on earth like Jesus!

God's plan all along was for Jesus to provide the way for us to live with Him in heaven forever someday. Our sin problem needed an answer. God knew we could not pay the price for our sins on our own. He sent his Son, Jesus, to earth to pay the price for our sins instead.

Jesus is the Son of God. He never sinned or did anything wrong. That is why He is the only one who is worthy and able to pay the price for our sins. Jesus paid that price on a cross!

God felt sad to see Jesus suffer and die on the cross. He also felt sad to be separated from us. It hurts to be separated from those we love. That is why God made a way to be with us again. He knew Jesus' death was the only way to solve our sin problem. Only Jesus could make a way to join Him in heaven someday.

What color is the cross on this page? This red cross reminds us of the color of Jesus' blood. Jesus loves us so much that He willingly died on the cross to forgive our sins. That's a great love! How do you know someone loves you?

The best part of God's story is Jesus did not stay dead! After three days, He came back to life! Many people saw Jesus alive, and then He went to heaven. How do you think people felt when they saw Jesus alive after He died? The Easter story celebrates how Jesus came alive. What do you remember from that story?

Jesus paid the punishment for sin by dying on the cross. Then He proved He is the Son of God by rising from the dead! Only Jesus can do a miracle like that. Jesus took away our sin and gave us grace and forgiveness instead. When He came back to life, Jesus showed us He is the only way to heaven.

This picture reminds us Jesus did not stay dead. His tomb is empty! We praise and honor Jesus because—

HE IS ALIVE!

Look closely at this heart. How is it different from the heart earlier in the book? Jesus can change a dirty and broken heart and make it clean and healthy.

GOD HAS A PLAN FOR YOU!

To know God and have Him heal your heart, you need to:

- ADMIT that you sin and ask Jesus to forgive you
- BELIEVE that Jesus willingly died on the cross for your sins and came back to life
- INVITE Jesus to live in your life as your Savior and follow Him
- ACCEPT by faith Jesus' free gift of life forever in heaven

When we believe what the Bible says about Jesus and ask Him to forgive our sins, a wonderful thing happens. Let's place our hand on the clean heart. Jesus heals our dirty, broken heart. God takes away our sin and shame.

We cannot see the Savior Jesus, but when we believe in Him, His powerful Spirit will come and live in our lives. His Spirit works in us and gives us peace. When our sin problem is forgiven and Jesus' Spirit lives in us, we know that we will live in heaven someday!

When we believe in Jesus and His Spirit lives in us, we become a child of God. Just like when we were born into our family, we are now born into God's family.

When we are a child of God, we still do things that are not right. When we do wrong things, we should ask Jesus to forgive us. He forgives us whenever we ask. His Spirit helps us make right choices, even when it is hard. Sometimes we don't want to do what is right, like sharing, obeying our parents, or having a good attitude. When it is hard, we can ask Jesus to help us do what is right. We all need help to learn how to serve and follow Jesus.

The Bible says when we are a child of God, He promises to NEVER leave us! We will never be alone. That's awesome, because life can be hard for kids and grown-ups. When we are afraid, we can ask Jesus to help us be brave. Can you describe something hard where we need God's help?

Do you see all the plants on this page? What color are they? Plants are green because they are alive and growing. It takes time for things to grow. Have you ever wondered why it takes time for a seed to grow? God gives the seed important things to grow into a healthy plant—water, sun, and soil. Have you ever planted a seed and waited for it to grow?

GOD HAS A PLAN FOR YOU! God wants His children to grow too. We need to grow in our understanding of Jesus. That means we need to know more about Him. The more we know Jesus and understand the Bible, the more we honor Him in how we think and act. Acting like Jesus shows we are growing. Growing in Jesus takes time.

God gives His children important things to help us grow in Jesus. What ways can you think of to learn more about Jesus? We grow in Jesus by going to church with other kids and grown-ups who love Him. We grow in Jesus by singing songs of praise.

We grow in Jesus by reading the Bible and memorizing Bible verses. We grow in Jesus by praying to Him. What is prayer? Prayer is simply talking with God.

We can tell God anything.
We can thank God for anything.
He always listens to us because we
matter to Him! He loves to listen to us and speak to us. He speaks to us through the Bible and His Spirit. Is there something you would like to tell God right now? Let's stop right now and talk with God together.

God wants you to share the story of Jesus with others. You can tell your friends about Him and invite them to church. You can pray for your friends. You can even pray for your enemies.

Is it easy to love people who are not nice to us? It's not, but God loves us when we are not very nice. He helps us learn to love others in the same way. God's Spirit gives us courage and power to do what is right when it is hard. If we are kind to others, they may want to know Jesus too!

GOD LOVES ALL
PEOPLE JUST LIKE HE LOVES YOU.
There are many ways to help others know about Jesus. It makes Him happy when we love Him so much, we want to share His story with our friends and neighbors. Can you name a friend who might like to know about Jesus?

Can you see your reflection in a mirror? When you look at yourself, do you see yourself the same way God does? When God looks at you, He loves you because you are His special and unique creation! He made you just the way He wants you to be.

We don't know what will happen tomorrow, but God does.
God knows all things.
GOD HAS A PLAN FOR YOU!

The title of this book asks, *"What is God's Plan for Me?"* God's plan is for you to know and love Jesus. That happens when you believe what the Bible says about Jesus, ask forgiveness for your sins, and follow Him. Choosing to follow Jesus and to believe in Him is something each person decides for himself. No one can do it for another person.

Do you believe God made you? Do you believe God loves you? You can talk to God right now and ask Him to help you understand His plan for you. Welcome God into your life today and choose to believe —

GOD HAS A PLAN FOR YOU!

VOCABULARY WORDS
AND DEFINITIONS

CHURCH
A gathering of people who believe in Jesus and want to worship and follow Him.

FAITH
Belief in God even though you cannot see Him.

FORGIVE
To cancel a debt; or let go of an offense.

HONOR
Show respect and please God in our thoughts and actions.

MIRACLE
An extraordinary event showing the power of God.

PUNISHMENT
The payment required for sin.

SHAME
An embarrassing or painful feeling caused by doing something wrong.

WILLING
Ready to perform or join in gladly and cheerfully.

DISOBEY
To ignore God and reject what He says in the Bible.

FEAR
To be afraid of someone or something.

GUILT
Being responsible for doing something wrong.

HOPE
To look forward to something with expectation and confidence.

PEACE
A quiet and calm feeling.

SAVIOR
A person who rescues someone and/or takes their place.

TOMB
A place where a dead body is buried.

WORTHY
A person who has great value.

SUGGESTED PRAYERS

CHILD'S PRAYER

If your child is ready to make a personal decision to accept Jesus after reading *What is God's Plan for Me?*, you may want to guide them with a prayer similar to the one below.

Dear Jesus, I believe that you made me and love me. I know I have disobeyed you by thinking and doing things against your directions. I am sorry. Please forgive my sins. I believe that you died on the cross and came to life again to save me from these sins. I invite you to live in my life as my Savior and friend. I accept the free gift of living in heaven with you someday. Help me follow you in my life every day. Amen.

ADULT'S PRAYER

This prayer is a guide to support you in praying for the children you love as they wrestle with the gospel message. You may want to insert your child's name in the blanks.

Lord, I desire to raise _____ in a way that pleases you and leads them to you. I know that even if they say all the right things and do what looks right, that doesn't mean their hearts are in the right place. But you know their hearts, Lord, and you can change them. I pray that You will draw _____'s heart close to you. I pray that in your right time, _____ will recognize and fully comprehend that they have sinned and are separated from you. I pray they also know that you love them so much that you gave your only Son, Jesus, that whoever believes in Him will not die but have everlasting life in heaven. I know, Father, that you desire all men to be saved and come to a knowledge of the truth, so I pray, in faith and according to your will, and ask you to bring _____ to a saving knowledge of you! May they, through faith, accept your gift of salvation. Help me to pray faithfully for them and follow you closely in my own life. Thank you, Lord. Amen

WHAT IS GOD'S PLAN FOR ME? teaches children different topics related to the gospel message. The topics and supporting Bible verses below correspond to each double-spread page of the story. Use them as a reference guide.

CREATION

EXODUS 20:11, "*For in six days the Lord made the heavens and the earth, the sea, and all that is in them.*"

GENESIS 1:27, "*So God created man in his own image, in the image of God he created him; male and female he created them.*"

HEAVEN

REVELATION 21:3-4, "*Now the dwelling of God is with man… He will wipe every tear from their eyes. There will be no more death or mourning or crying or pain…*"

JOHN 14:2, "*In my Father's house are many rooms… I am going to prepare a place for you.*"

SIN

ROMANS 3:23, "*For all have sinned and fall short of the glory of God.*"

ROMANS 5:12, "*Therefore, just as sin entered the world through one man, and death through sin, and in this way death came to all men, because all sinned*"

CONSEQUENCE OF SIN

ROMANS 6:23, "*For the wages of sin is death, but the gift of God is eternal life in Christ Jesus our Lord.*"

EPHESIANS 2:8-9, "*For it is by grace you have been saved, through faith – and this not from yourselves, it is the gift of God – not by works, so that no one can boast.*"

BIRTH AND LIFE OF JESUS

LUKE 1:30-32, "But the angel said to her, 'Do not be afraid, Mary, you have found favor with God. You will be with child and give birth to a son, and you are to give him the name Jesus. He will be great and will be called the Son of the Most High.'"

1 JOHN 4:9-10, "This is how God showed his love among us: He sent his one and only Son into the world that we might live through him."

2 CORINTHIANS 5:21, "God made him who had no sin to be sin for us, so that in him we might become the righteousness of God."

DEATH OF JESUS

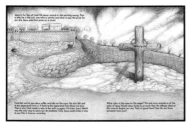

ISAIAH 53:5, "But he was pierced for our transgressions, he was crushed for our iniquities; the punishment that brought us peace was upon him, and by his wounds we are healed."

ROMANS 5:8, "But God demonstrates his own love for us in this: While we were still sinners, Christ died for us."

JOHN 3:16, "For God so loved the world that he gave his one and only Son, that whoever believes in him shall not perish but have eternal life."

RESURRECTION OF JESUS

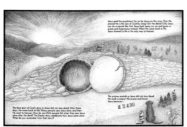

1 CORINTHIANS 15:3-6, "...that Christ died for our sins according to the Scriptures, that he was buried, that he was raised on the third day according to the Scriptures, and that he appeared to Peter, and then to the Twelve. After that, he appeared to more than five hundred of the brothers at the same time."

MATTHEW 28:5, "The angel said to the women, 'Do not be afraid, for I know that you are looking for Jesus, who was crucified. He is not here; he has risen, just as he said.'"

LUKE 24:46, "...This is what is written: The Christ will suffer and rise from the dead on the third day, and repentance and forgiveness of sins will be preached in his name to all nations..."

SALVATION

JOHN 14:6, *"Jesus answered, 'I am the way and the truth and the life. No one comes to the Father except through me."*

ROMANS 10:9, *"That if you confess with your mouth, 'Jesus is Lord,' and believe in your heart that God raised him from the dead, you will be saved."*

ACTS 1:8, *"But you will receive power when the Holy Spirit comes on you; and you will be my witnesses in Jerusalem, and in all Judea and Samaria, and to the ends of the earth."*

HOLY SPIRIT

JOHN 1:12, *"Yet, to all who received him, to those who believed in his name, he gave the right to become children of God."*

DEUTERONOMY 31:6, *"Be strong and courageous. Do not be afraid or terrified because of them, for the Lord your God goes with you; he will never leave you nor forsake you."*

JOHN 14:26, *"But the Helper, the Holy Spirit, whom the Father will send in my name, will teach you all things and remind you of everything that I have told you."*

GROW IN JESUS

2 PETER 3:18, *"But grow in the grace and knowledge of our Lord and Savior Jesus Christ."*

EPHESIANS 4:32, *"Be kind and compassionate to one another, forgiving each other, just as in Christ God forgave you."*

GALATIANS 5:22, *"But the fruit of the Spirit is love, joy, peace, patience, kindness, goodness, faithfulness, gentleness, and self-control..."*

GROW IN FAITH

COLOSSIANS 2:6-8, "So then, just as you received Christ Jesus as Lord, continue to live in him, rooted and built up in him, strengthened in the faith as you were taught and overflowing with thankfulness."

ROMANS 12:9-10, "Love must be sincere. Hate what is evil; cling to what is good. Be devoted to one another in brotherly love. Honor one another above yourself."

I THESSALONIANS 5:16, "Be joyful always; pray continually; give thanks in all circumstances for this is God's will for you in Christ Jesus."

EVANGELISM

MATTHEW 28:19-20, "Therefore go and make disciples of all nations, baptizing them in the name of the Father and of the Son and of the Holy Spirit, and teaching them to obey everything I have commanded you. And surely I am with you always, to the very end of the age."

ROMANS 1:16, "I am not ashamed of the gospel, because it is the power of God for the salvation of everyone who believes..."

I JOHN 4:11, "Dear friends, since God so loved us, we also ought to love one another."

FUTURE

PSALM 139:14, "I praise you because I am fearfully and wonderfully made; your works are wonderful, I know that full well."

JEREMIAH 29:11-12, "For I know the plans I have for you, declares the Lord, plans to prosper you and not to harm you, plans to give you hope and a future. Then you will call upon me and come and pray to me, and I will listen to you. You will seek me and find me when you seek me with all your heart."

EPHESIANS 5:1, "Be imitators of God, therefore, as dearly loved children and live a life of love, just as Christ loved us and gave himself up for us..."

Use the geology, flora, and fauna notes below as an educational guide. Ask children to compare the similarities and differences in their geographic locationto the ones illustrated in **WHAT IS GOD'S PLAN FOR ME?** Children are encouraged to search and find each unique creation of God explained below.

THREE SISTERS MOUNTAINS: Three dormant stratovolcanoes in the Cascade Mountain Range of the western United States. They are located near the rodeo town of Sisters, Oregon. The Three Sisters are all over 10,000 ft. in elevation and are named Faith (north mountain), Hope (middle mountain), and Charity (south mountain). North and Middle Sister are close to each other and South Sister is set apart from them.There are active glaciers found on the Three Sisters Mountains. Many popular hiking trails traverse these stunning mountains.

MOUNT JEFFERSON: A dormant stratovolcano in the center of the Cascade Mountain Range of the western United States. Mt. Jefferson is the second tallest mountain in Oregon with an elevation of 10,495 ft. and was named after President Thomas Jefferson. Mt. Jefferson has four active glaciers. It is extremely rugged and is one of the most difficult mountains in the Cascades to hike. Common wildlife found in the Mount Jefferson Wilderness include deer, elk, black bear, mountain goats, coyotes, wolves, cougars, and bald eagles.

MOUNT HOOD: A dormant stratovolcano located 50 miles southeast of Portland, Oregon and along the Columbia River. Mt. Hood is the tallest mountain in the Oregon Cascade Mountains in the western United States and stands 11,249 ft. in elevation. It has eleven active glaciers and vents sulfurous steam near its summit. Timberline Lodge on Mt. Hood is a popular place to snowboard and ski. Mt. Hood was named after a British admiral, Lord Samuel Hood.

DESCHUTES RIVER: The Deschutes River is a major tributary river that flows from the Cascade Mountains north 252 miles to the Columbia River. It provides needed farming irrigation to the semiarid climate of the high desert of Central Oregon. The Deschutes River has scenic waterfalls and many people enjoy Class I to V rapids for exciting whitewater rafting and kayaking. Fly fishing is another popular recreational activity on the Deschutes River.

CROOKED RIVER CANYON: Central Oregon has many steep sided canyons. The Crooked River Canyon Gorge is a breath-taking scenic view off of Hwy 97 that is up to 500 ft. deep and surrounded by steep cliffs of volcanic basalt.

CLINE BUTTES: Cline Buttes are three dome-shaped low mountain peaks (4,101 ft. in elevation) located in the heart of Central Oregon. The Deschutes River runs next to Cline Buttes and spills over the beautiful Cline Falls creating a popular swimming location. The sandy soil of Cline Buttes makes them perfect for popular recreational trails used for hiking, running, cycling, motor biking, and horseback riding. A magnificent view of the Cascade Mountain Range can be seen from the summit.

SMITH ROCK STATE PARK: Smith Rock State Park is one of the most popular state parks in Central Oregon. It is famous for its sheer cliffs of basalt, which are ideal for rock climbing. It has scenic views of deep river canyons, breath-taking hiking trails, and rocks for bouldering. The Crooked River flows around Smith Rock State Park. Misery Ridge is the name of the most popular hiking trail with viewpoints along its route that overlook famous rock-climbing faces, the Crooked River, and the Cascade Mountains. Mule deer, river otters, and rattle snakes are often sighted at the park.

BUNCHGRASS: A native grass that grows in the semiarid climate of the high desert of Central Oregon and needs very little water to survive. It is a low, nutritious grass that grows in a small clump, or bunch, that is eaten by a variety of wildlife (such as mule deer and elk). Bunchgrass is also used for livestock grazing by open range cattle ranchers.

WESTERN JUNIPER TREE: A Juniper tree that is a native coniferous tree to the Pacific Northwest with needle-like leaves and clusters of small blue berries. They grow in the wide-open spaces of the Central Oregon high desert and are low and spreading. As the tree grows slowly over time its trunk becomes gnarled and twisted. The Juniper gives off a strong aroma when it rains. Its twisted wood is often used to make unique furniture

PLUMELESS THISTLE: A bulb thistle that has a purple flower head and wide prickly leaves and stems. They can grow up to five feet tall. The Plumeless Thistle is an invasive weed that grows in the fields and forests around the high desert of Central Oregon.

KINCAID'S LUPINE: A beautiful flowering Lupine that grows throughout the Pacific Northwest and can be found on many of the Cascade mountain hiking trails. The flowers on Kincaid's Lupine are fragrant and range in color from bluish or purple to yellowish or creamy white. It is a threatened plant.

LILY OF THE VALLEY: A fragrant spring blooming plant that grows in the northern temperate zone. The flowers are petite, white, and dainty.

MONARCH BUTTERFLY: The North American Monarch Butterfly is an insect that has bright orange and black wings. It makes an amazing two-way annual migration of up to 3,000 miles one way. They leave their summer breeding ground in the northern United States and Canada and travel to their winter grounds in southwestern Mexico. The Monarch travels farther on its migration than any other butterfly in the world.

PACIFIC TREEFROG: The Pacific Treefrog is the most common frog in Oregon. Adult treefrogs measure two inches in length and vary in color from a bronze brown to a light green. They can be found in many trees and around damp vegetation.

WESTERN SCRUB-JAY: The Western Scrub-Jay, also known as the Long-tailed Jay, is often confused with the "Blue Jay" which belong to a different family of birds. The Western Scrub-Jay is thought to be an intelligent bird because it stores up food in various locations. It is also known as a sort of "bully" bird, picking on smaller song birds. Their diet includes fruit, insects, rodents, frogs, and eggs and nestlings of smaller song birds. The Western Scrub-Jay also enjoys eating the juniper berries found on Western Juniper trees.

ABOUT THE AUTHOR

Diane Hannay is an adventurous wife, mother of two adult children, spiritual mentor, and disciple of Jesus Christ. She is an educational leader with a Master of Education from Cedarville University. Her thirty-year career in education has included titles of author, speaker, instructional coach, elementary administrator, classroom teacher, and homeschool mom. She specializes in mentoring others to live fully committed to God. In her spare time, you may find Diane writing, traveling, gardening, and enjoying God's beautiful creation in her home state of Oregon.

Visit Diane's website at www.dianehannay.org for more exciting resources to support *What is God's Plan for Me?* Follow Diane on Instagram @mentor–heart for updates.

ABOUT THE ILLUSTRATOR

Scarlet Vandenbos fell in love with drawing at the age of two and rarely goes a day without putting pencil or brush to paper. She studied art and education in college, but most of what she learned about art was from her father, Bruce Day, who was a full-time artist and illustrator. This is the third book she has illustrated, and she hopes to bring glory to Jesus with every line and brushstroke. Scarlet lives with her husband and two boys in the picturesque state of Oregon.